Rookie
Read-About® Science

What Is Gravity?

By Lisa Trumbauer

Consultants
David Larwa
National Science Consultant

Nanci R. Vargus, Ed.D.
Assistant Professor of Literacy
University of Indianapolis
Indianapolis, Indiana

Children's Press®
A Division of Scholastic Inc.
New York   Toronto   London   Auckland   Sydney
Mexico City   New Delhi   Hong Kong
Danbury, Connecticut

Designer: Herman Adler Design
Photo Researcher: Caroline Anderson
The photo on the cover shows a girl catching a baseball.

Library of Congress Cataloging-in-Publication Data

Trumbauer, Lisa, 1963-
  What is gravity? / by Lisa Trumbauer.
      p. cm. — (Rookie read-about science)
Includes index.
Summary: A simple introduction to gravity, describing what it is and giving
some effects of this force.
  ISBN 0-516-23448-X (lib. bdg.)   0-516-25844-3 (pbk.)
  1. Gravity—Juvenile literature. [1. Gravity.] I. Title. II. Series.
QC178.T78 2003
531'.14—dc22

                                                                2003019064

CHILDREN'S PRESS, and ROOKIE READ-ABOUT®,
and associated logos are trademarks and or registered trademarks
of Scholastic Library Publishing. SCHOLASTIC and associated logos
are trademarks and or registered trademarks of Scholastic Inc.

1 2 3 4 5 6 7 8 9 10 R 13 12 11 10 09 08 07 06 05 04

What happens when you throw a basketball at a net?

The ball goes up. Then it comes back down through the net.

Swoosh!

It falls to the ground.

Can you think of other things that go up and then come down?

A diver jumps on the end of a diving board.

She flies up into the air. Then she turns and goes back down into the water.

A baseball player hits a ball
high into the air. The ball
comes back to the ground.

Someone catches it.
You're out!

Things fall to the ground because of gravity. Gravity pulls things down.

You cannot see gravity, but it is always there.

A skier can zoom down a
hill because of gravity.

You can zip down a slide because of gravity.

Gravity pulls on everything.

Why does rain fall down
instead of up?

Because of gravity!

Gravity pulls harder on heavier objects. Pick up a doll.

Now try to lift up a friend.
Is your friend lighter or
heavier than the doll?

Gravity pulls down very hard on heavy weights. The weight lifter has to work hard to lift them.

Gravity always pulls things downward. Apples fall straight down from a tree.

What happens if you throw
a snowball sideways? It will
still fall down.

What if you throw a ball
straight up? It will still
fall down.

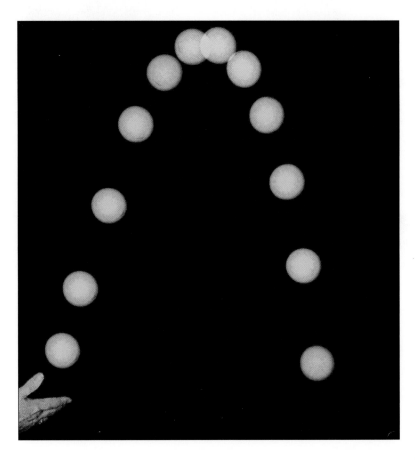

You can test gravity.

Place a ball on a ramp.
Let it go. Which way
does it roll—up or down?

Jump up. You will always come back down.

Gravity has its grip on you!

Words You Know

basketball

diving board

ramp   skier

weight lifter

Index

About the Author

Lisa Trumbauer has written a dozen books about the physical sciences and dozens more about other branches of science. She has also edited science programs for teachers of young children. Lisa lives in New Jersey with one dog, two cats, and her husband, Dave.

Photo Credits

Photographs © 2004: Corbis Images: 29 (Chris Carroll), 13 (Joe McBride), 7 (Michael Neveux), 3 (Royalty Free); Folio, Inc./Al Messerschmidt: 9, 30 right; Index Stock Imagery/Lynn Stone: 22; Network Aspen/Jeffrey Aaronson: 14, 31 top right; Omni-Photo Communications: 15 (Yvonne Bassett), 18 (Catrina Genovese); PhotoDisc/Getty Images/Geoff Manasse: cover; PhotoEdit: 19 (Myrleen Ferguson Cate), 6, 25 (Tony Freeman), 21, 31 bottom (Spencer Grant), 26, 31 top left (David Young-Wolff); Stock Boston/Bob Daemmrich: 10; Superstock, Inc.: 5, 30 left (Francisco Cruz), 11 (Kevin Radford); Taxi/Getty Images/Jim Cummins: 17; Visuals Unlimited/Jack Ballard: 24.